W9-BRS-174

———————— *Ancient Civilizations* ————————

Published by Creative Education
P.O. Box 227, Mankato, Minnesota 56002
Creative Education is an imprint of
THE CREATIVE COMPANY
www.thecreativecompany.us

Design and production by CHRISTINE VANDERBEEK
Art direction by RITA MARSHALL

Printed in the United States of America

PHOTOGRAPHS BY Alamy (Ian M Butterfield [Rome],
imagebroker, Lebrecht Music and Arts Photo Library),
Corbis (Atlantide Phototravel, Morton Beebe, Christie's
Images, Ken Kaminesky, Alfredo Dagli Orti/The Art
Archive, Gianni Dagli Orti, Paul Seheult/Westend61,
Tarker, Roger Wood), Getty Images (DEA/A. DAGLI
ORTI/De Agostini), SuperStock (Album/Oronoz/
Album, Album/Prisma/Album, Piotr Ciesla/age
fotostock, DeAgostini, Elio Lombardo/age fotostock,
Pantheon, Pixtal)

COPYRIGHT © 2015 CREATIVE EDUCATION
International copyright reserved in all countries. No part
of this book may be reproduced in any form without
written permission from the publisher.

LIBRARY OF CONGRESS
CATALOGING-IN-PUBLICATION DATA
Bodden, Valerie.
Rome / Valerie Bodden.
p. cm. — (Ancient civilizations)
Includes bibliographical references and index.
SUMMARY: A historical overview of the Roman civiliza-
tion from the perspectives of the social classes, from the
senators to the plebeians, including the Italian empire's
growth and decline.

ISBN 978-1-60818-394-4
1. Rome—Civilization—Juvenile literature. I. Title.

DG77.B67 2014
937'.63—dc23   2013032514

ccss: RI.5.1, 2, 3, 5, 6, 8, 9; RH.6-8.4, 5, 6, 7, 8, 9

FIRST EDITION
9 8 7 6 5 4 3 2 1

CREATIVE C EDUCATION

ROME

VALERIE BODDEN

TABLE OF CONTENTS

INTRODUCTION

Rome began as a small city near the Tiber River in central Italy in the eighth century B.C. Its people were humble farmers who also formed a powerful army. Over the course of 10 centuries, that army brought much of Europe, western Asia, and northern Africa under Roman control. As the Romans conquered new lands, they brought their culture along.

In the thousand-plus years of its existence, Rome was ruled by three distinct governments. At first, the city functioned as a monarchy, with a king as its head. By 509 B.C., the monarchy had collapsed. It was replaced by a republic in which citizens took part in electing rulers and passing laws. In 27 B.C., the republic gave way to an empire ruled by an emperor with absolute power.

Roman emperors such as Hadrian built structures in the capital city that remain today.

Although Rome's government changed over the centuries, its social order did not. Throughout its history, Roman society was clearly divided. The first division was between citizens and noncitizens. "Citizens" at first meant free residents of the city of Rome. Later, citizenship was extended to any free inhabitant of the entire empire. For men, citizenship brought with it a number of rights, including the ability to serve in the government. It also required service in the army when needed.

Not all citizens were considered equal, however. Female citizens did not have the same right to participate in government as did males. And even a male citizen's position in society was legally determined by the census, or population survey. The census registered citizens' reports of their wealth, age, and family heritage. This information was then used to separate citizens into specific orders, or classes. These orders

ROMAN EMPIRE CIRCA A.D. 117

determined a citizen's eligibility for government service, his position in the army, and his obligation to pay a share of taxes.

At the top of the social order were the wealthy senatorial and *equestrian* classes. Although these classes made up only a small percentage of the population, they held nearly all the power in the government. They also served as military officers and held Rome's many priestly offices. The plebeians, or common people, who formed the majority of the Roman population, had little power. They were Rome's laborers—its farmers, merchants, and artisans. Ranking even below the plebeians were slaves and freedmen (ex-slaves).

Despite such clear social distinctions, Romans of one class frequently interacted with members of the other classes—though never as equals. And, although not common, some people of the lower classes did manage to improve their standing in society.

Ancient Greek stories inspired much of the artwork that later Roman citizens enjoyed.

RULERS OF THE ROMAN WORLD

For more than 200 years after its founding, Rome was ruled by a series of kings. During this time, Rome developed from a rustic village into a large city, with a public center, temples, and trade. Class divisions soon became apparent. Wealthy men were named as advisers to the king. These so-called "fathers" of the state assumed the title "patricians" (after the Latin word for "father," *pater*). The title of patrician was passed down through the generations of a family. Anyone who did not belong to the patrician class was considered a plebeian. Although the kings held absolute authority, their patrician advisers formed a council known as the Senate.

Roman senators eventually met in the Palace of the Senators, also called the Capitol.

In 509 B.C., the Roman king was driven from office, either by the wealthy elite in Rome or by a foreign power. A republic took the monarchy's place. In a republic, the people participate in the government through voting. In Rome, all male citizens had the right to vote. But not all citizens' votes counted equally. For many votes, citizens were divided into groups called centuries. Centuries were formed on the basis of wealth and age. Although there were fewer wealthy people than poor people, wealthier citizens were granted more centuries. Each century cast one vote in the election, based on the majority vote of that century's citizens. Because the wealthiest citizens controlled more centuries than the poorest, the wealthy had a greater say in the government.

Each year, voters elected a number of public officials, known as magistrates. Magistrates oversaw the republic's cities, courts, roads, finances, and army. There were many levels of magistrates, and many politicians worked their way up through the ranks, serving in each position for a one-year term. Two magistrates known as consuls served as the head of the government.

At first, only patricians could serve as magistrates, but later, plebeians gained governmental positions as well. In general, however, only the wealthy became magistrates. Since magistrates did not receive payment for their service, only those who already had money could afford to hold such positions.

After serving his first year as a magistrate, a man usually became a member of the Senate for life. The Senate discussed new legislation proposed by the consuls. It then advised the consuls of which legislation to bring before the people for a vote. Throughout the period of the republic, the Senate grew more powerful.

Then, in 88 B.C., Rome fell into a series of civil wars. The wars led to the fall of the republic in 27 B.C., when Caesar Augustus became Rome's first emperor. From the time of Augustus on, emperors held absolute authority in the Roman Empire. Soon, the Roman people lost their right to vote. The power of the Senate also declined over time, as emperors handpicked loyal supporters for the most important posts.

Did You Know?

THE WALLS OF

WEALTHY ROMAN

HOMES WERE

OFTEN COVERED

WITH **FRESCOES**,

WHILE **MOSAICS**

OFTEN DECORATED

THE FLOORS.

Only a magistrate was permitted to sit on a curule chair, a symbol of legal authority.

ROMAN LEGEND HELD

THAT THE CITY OF

ROME WAS FOUNDED

BY TWINS NAMED

ROMULUS AND REMUS,

WHO WERE RAISED BY

A FEMALE WOLF.

No matter how much power they held in the government, the senatorial class remained at the top of the social order throughout Rome's history. But as the power of the Senate decreased, that of the next social order—the equestrians—grew. During the empire, many equestrians were recruited into the *imperial* government. Because of their increased status, many moved up to the senatorial order.

Other equestrians spent their days managing powerful trade, shipping, or banking enterprises. Members of the senatorial class, on the other hand, were officially forbidden from participating in business, although they often invested their money in business ventures. Both senators and equestrians also owned large areas of farmland. They often left the management of the farm to slaves or *tenant* farmers and simply collected the profits from it.

Since they were not officially engaged in business, senators spent much of their time campaigning for office. Once elected, they spent their days carrying out the duties of that office. In addition to their official duties, many wealthy citizens served as patrons, or protectors, of members of the lower class, who were known as the patrons' clients. The patron assisted his clients with money, food, or legal aid. In return, the clients provided services to the patron and voted for him. In addition to interacting with lower-class citizens in a patron-client relationship, wealthy Romans also mingled with people of all classes at the public baths, where they went to socialize, exercise, and bathe.

Even as they mixed with members of the lower class, Rome's upper-class citizens were set apart by their dress. Roman men of all classes wore a tunic—a belted shirt that hung to the knees. But on top of the tunic, upper class citizens wore a toga, or a large piece of cloth wrapped around the body. A toga's design indicated a person's social status. Legally, only senators could wear a white toga with a wide purple stripe at the bottom. Equestrian togas were marked by a narrower purple stripe. Women wore a longer tunic called a stola. Over this they often wore a shawl known as a *palla*.

Although dwellings at the time of Rome's founding were simple huts, the wealthy soon began to erect luxurious homes. Known as a *domus*, a Roman home was large enough for a couple, their children, relatives, and slaves. At the center of the home was an atrium, or courtyard, where the wealthy homeowner received guests and clients.

Many wealthy citizens also had vacation villas in the country. These villas were often even more luxurious than the city domus, with *colonnaded* gardens, bubbling fountains, and elegant statues. When a senator needed a break from his official duties in the city, he might travel to his villa in a

The bronze Capitoline Wolf statue was made in northern Italy in the sixth century B.C.

litter carried by his slaves.

Wealthy citizens often hosted elaborate dinner parties at their homes. Guests reclined on couches as they were served extravagant dishes that proved their host's wealth. Exotic foods such as ostrich and flamingo might be served alongside eggs, olives, seafood, fruits, and cakes made with honey. Always aware of one another's social status, hosts would seat the guests of the highest social standing in the place of honor at the center couch. They might serve lower-class guests, such as clients, poorer-quality food.

Roman dinner parties might include women, but otherwise, women were generally excluded from public life. Although women were considered citizens, they did not have the right to vote or to serve in political office. When an upper-class woman did venture into public, she had to keep her head covered with her palla. At home, women remained under the authority of the oldest male

Did You Know?

ROMAN GIRLS WERE

OFTEN MARRIED BY

AGE 12. BOYS MIGHT

GET MARRIED AT

THE AGE OF 14, BUT

MANY WERE OLDER.

in the family, known as the paterfamilias. A woman's job extended to caring for the children and making clothing. In many wealthy households, however, these tasks were taken care of by slaves. Little is known about the lives of women in ancient Rome, since men rarely wrote about women. Most women had little or no education, so they left no written record of their own lives.

Boys and young men from upper-class families, on the other hand, underwent a lengthy education. A wealthy young boy was usually instructed by a tutor—often an educated slave from Greece. The boy would study history, geography, Greek, public speaking, and literature. Around the age of 12, a boy might go on to study *grammar*, literature, mathematics, and astronomy under a teacher known as a grammaticus. A few years later, some boys began to study public speaking with a *rhetor* to prepare for careers in law or politics.

Clues about Roman women's lives can be found in surviving artwork such as frescoes.

SERVING GODS AND COUNTRY

Rome's upper classes not only controlled its political power but also directed its religious and military life. The Romans believed that different deities, or gods, controlled different parts of human life. Jupiter, for example, was thought to protect the city of Rome. Juno watched over women and childbirth, and Mars ruled over wars. As the Romans conquered new territories, they also began to worship the deities of the peoples they conquered. During imperial times, many emperors were declared gods after their deaths.

Religion was an important part of daily life for all Romans. Roman homes had an ***altar*** for daily worship of various gods. Although each family performed its own ceremonies, the Romans also believed that it was

Romans made the Greek-Egyptian god Serapis (hybrid of Zeus and Osiris) even more popular.

important to have priests lead religious ceremonies on behalf of the state. It was the priests' job to keep the gods happy so that Rome could prosper.

Rome had a number of priests, each with a different job, such as carrying out certain rituals or overseeing worship of a single deity. Priests were not set apart from the rest of society. Instead, many priests were elected or appointed from Rome's upper-class families. Like most other public offices, the office of priest was an unpaid position, but it brought with it social status. Magistrates also performed priestly functions such as sacrificing cattle, sheep, or goats to the gods, in addition to their governmental duties.

Most of Rome's 200 or so priests were grouped into four colleges, each of which carried out its own duties. The head of the priests was known as the pontifex maximus, or chief priest. During the monarchy, the king served as the chief priest. Later, the emperor held this title.

The most important priestly college was known as the college of the pontiffs. Pontiffs presided over festivals and sacrifices. As they

Did You Know?

———

ROME'S LARGEST ARENA

FOR **GLADIATOR**

GAMES WAS THE

COLOSSEUM, WHICH

OPENED IN A.D. 80

WITH 100 DAYS

OF GAMES.

———

carried out these religious acts, priests had to pay careful attention to detail. The Romans believed that if the priests said even one word wrong, the ritual might not please the gods. The college of the pontiffs also included the Vestal Virgins. These six priestesses were the only women to serve in a temple in Rome. They served Vesta, goddess of the hearth and home.

While the college of pontiffs performed specific rituals, the college of *augurs* looked for signs from the gods to help make political and military decisions. These signs were generally to be found in the flight of birds or in birds' eating habits. Another college, known as the priesthood of Fifteen, interpreted books containing ancient prophesies. The college of the feasters oversaw feasts for the gods.

In the first century A.D., a new religion also began to take hold in the Roman world. *Christianity* spread slowly at first, and many Christians were persecuted for their refusal to take part in rituals honoring Roman gods. Members of the upper classes mistrusted Christianity

Beneath the Colosseum's floor were two levels of cages and tunnels called the hypogeum.

MORE THAN 250,000

MILES (402,336 KM)

OF ROADS CONNECTED

THE PROVINCES TO

THE CENTER OF

POWER IN ROME.

because of its appeal to lower-class citizens. By the third century, however, Christianity had broken through barriers of class. The emperor Constantine declared himself a Christian, and in A.D. 313, he issued the Edict of Milan, a statement that called for an end to persecution of Christians. Christianity soon became the main religion in Rome. New priesthoods, such as bishops and deacons, were established in the young church.

In addition to being a religious society, Rome was also a militaristic one. From its founding, Rome relied on a strong military to conquer new territories and defend its borders. Military conquests brought wealth to Rome in the form of *booty* as well as in taxes collected from conquered peoples. In fact, Rome was able to gain so much income from taxes demanded of its provinces that by 167 B.C., citizens did not have to pay any direct taxes of their own.

During the republic, Rome's army functioned as a force of citizen-soldiers who were required to serve when needed. Men served with the same centuries in which they voted. In general, wealthy centuries were called up for service first, since they were able to afford better equipment for battle. In addition, as Rome's leaders, they had a bigger stake in its success. Lower-class centuries were also called upon when needed. Wealthy citizens of the equestrian order, who could purchase their own horses and equipment, served in the cavalry, which consisted of soldiers mounted on horses. Lower-class citizens made up the infantry, or foot soldiers. Consuls served as commanders of the army, with members of the Senate serving as generals under them.

Citizens were called to service only for a specific campaign, or series of battles against a single enemy. Once that campaign was done, the citizens could return home. Although this system of citizen-soldiers worked well at first, later battles were fought farther and farther from Rome, and soldiers had to spend a considerable amount of time traveling to battle. Sometimes it seemed that the wars would never end, with one fought upon another, so that citizens were often away from home for years at a time. For small farmers, such absence was devastating. They could not maintain their land and often had to sell or abandon it. The wealthy were then quick to scoop it up. Property ownership was a qualification for service in the army, so as more Romans lost their land, there were fewer men to call upon for army service.

In order to fill its ranks, the Roman army began to lower the minimum age for soldiers and to loosen the restriction on property ownership. When there still weren't enough soldiers, the army recruited volunteers. Many lower-class men were eager to join the army, which promised a wage as well as the possibility of booty.

Major roadways were paved with stones and crowned, or curved, to allow water to drain off.

It also offered a long-term job, with service lengths of 16 to 28 years. As a result, the army of citizen-soldiers was slowly transformed into a permanent, professional army during the empire.

The Roman army was the best-trained fighting force of its day. When not at war, soldiers spent their days getting in shape for battle with long marches carrying heavy packs. They ran, swam, and jumped ditches. Training also involved learning battle tactics and practicing with weapons. Roman soldiers carried short swords and javelins, or spears. They were protected by armor, helmets, and shields.

A Roman war camp functioned like a small, walled city. The camp might even contain luxuries, such as a bath and hearty meals of meat. Between battles, soldiers constructed public works such as roads and bridges. Some also started families. Although unmarried soldiers were not allowed to marry while in service, many had relationships

Did You Know?

THE ROMANS BUILT

AQUEDUCTS TO

CHANNEL WATER INTO

THEIR CITIES. MANY OF

THE AQUEDUCTS TOOK

THE FORM OF BRIDGES

OVER RIVERS.

with the women who lived near their camps. When his term of service was complete, a soldier might remain with his new family. During certain periods in Rome's history, retired soldiers were even granted land in the province where they had served. In this manner, the Roman way of life spread throughout the Roman world.

Land was not the only benefit soldiers received. Once a permanent army was formed, soldiers also began to receive regular pay. Officers received much higher salaries than did ordinary soldiers. From time to time, soldiers also received bonuses to celebrate notable events such as the crowning of a new emperor. At the end of their career, all soldiers also received a retirement bonus. Noncitizen soldiers from Rome's provinces could be granted citizenship when they retired. For wealthy army officers, a successful military career often led to a successful political one.

The Roman-built Pont du Gard aqueduct in France used the lower level as a road.

LIFE AMONG THE MASSES

The majority of Rome's citizens were plebeians, or commoners. Anyone who did not belong to an elite patrician family was considered a plebeian. Most plebeians were poor in comparison with the upper classes of Roman society.

Because they did not belong to the ruling classes of senators and equestrians, plebeians had little political power during the monarchy or the early years of the republic. In the fifth century B.C., plebeians began to demand more rights. By 287 B.C., they were allowed to hold important government offices. But only the few plebeians who had managed to become wealthy could take advantage of this right, since political offices were generally unpaid positions. The plebeians

Some rulers gave plebeians bread or grain to keep them from rioting against patricians.

elected their own magistrates (tribunes of the people) to represent their interests. They also formed the plebeian assembly, in which only plebeians could vote. The assembly met to pass laws and elect tribunes. During the empire, however, power was taken from all voters, including the plebeian assembly.

In addition to having less power than the elite classes, plebeians were also dealt with differently under Roman law. Until 445 B.C., plebeians were not allowed to marry patricians. Later, in the third century A.D., Roman law divided citizens into two groups. The upper classes—which included senators, equestrians, and army officers—were considered the *honestiores*, or "more honorable." They represented only 2 percent of the population. Everyone else was classified as the *humiliores*, or "more lowly." Punishments for humiliores convicted of a crime were much harsher than those for honestiores. Humiliores might face **crucifixion** or hard labor for a serious crime, while honestiores might only be exiled, or sent away, for the same crime.

The harsher punishments faced by Rome's

Did You Know?

THE ROMAN WRITER JUVENAL (C. A.D. 60–130) WROTE **SATIRES** ABOUT THE STRUGGLES OF ROME'S POOR AND THE PRIVILEGES OF THE RICH.

lower-class citizens reflected the belief of Rome's rulers that the senatorial and equestrian classes made a greater contribution to Roman society. Yet, the lower classes were essential to daily life in Rome, since they served (along with slaves) as its laborers, providing the goods and services the upper classes needed. Even as they purchased such goods and services, however, the Roman elite looked down on anyone who had to work to earn a living. Such a living was much humbler than that made by senators and equestrians. While a plebeian laborer might make three sesterces (a sesterce was a Roman coin) a day, a rich man might have land worth 4 million sesterces. And that land might earn him 550 sesterces a day.

Rome's plebeians were employed in nearly every job imaginable, from bricklayers to barbers, furniture makers to cart drivers. They were construction workers, butchers, shoemakers, bakers, cleaners, and teachers. Many plebeians worked as artisans, making jewelry, glasswork, pottery, and other handcrafted goods. Most artisans worked in small workshops, where they might labor

Plebeians labored constantly but had little in the way of material goods to show for it.

IN 195 B.C., ROMAN

WOMEN PROTESTED

THE CONTINUATION

OF A LAW BANNING

LUXURY ITEMS SUCH

AS JEWELRY AND

EXPENSIVE CLOTHING.

alongside slaves and freedmen. While some artisans created unique works, others performed the same tasks over and over again, working as part of an assembly line to create a final product. Although painters and sculptors exercised more creative freedom, they were considered to be on the same level as artisans. Upper-class Romans believed that the credit for a work of art should go to the person who requested and paid for it rather than to its creator. Thus, artists were seen as simple laborers.

Many artisans were also merchants. They produced their products at the back of their workshop and offered them for sale at the front. Sometimes they even lived in a room behind or above the shop. Many shops were crowded near the Roman Forum, or city center, and its surrounding streets, although over time officials strove to push such businesses to the edges of the city.

While the law was thought a suitable profession for upper-class men, doctors were considered laborers rather than skilled professionals. Many doctors were slaves or freedmen, often from Greece. Teaching positions, too, were usually held by freedmen.

The education of plebeian boys was much less extensive than that of an upper-class boy. A boy born to a poor family might attend a small school from the ages of 7 to 11. Then, rather than continuing his education, he went to work as an *apprentice*, often in his father's shop. Few girls went to school.

Although many plebeians lived and worked in Roman cities, the majority worked the land. A few owned their own farms, but most farmed rented land or worked as hired hands on the estates of wealthy landowners. Farming life was hard, and most farmers barely earned enough to feed their families. Over time, some farmers fled to Rome seeking work, but many were unsuccessful. As a result, the jobless rate was high. Many unemployed plebeians survived only because they were the clients of rich patrons, or protectors, who provided them with support.

Almost all Roman laborers were men. Like upper-class women, most plebeian women had little involvement in public life. They were expected to raise the children and see to the housework, including making the family's clothing. Some plebeian women did take jobs outside the home, however. They worked as dressmakers, hairdressers, teachers, shopkeepers, doctors, and midwives (women who help deliver babies).

The home a plebeian woman had to keep was much different from that of her upper-class counterparts. Most plebeians lived in cramped apartment buildings known as *insulae*. The insulae might be up to five or six stories tall, with shops on the ground floor and apartments above them. Often, several insulae filled a city block, with an

Upper-class women wore gems and gold, but lower-class "jewelry" was painted clay.

open courtyard in the middle. Although many insulae were owned by rich landlords who charged high rents, the buildings were poorly constructed. They were in constant danger of collapsing or being destroyed by fire. Insulae did not have running water, so those who lived there had to carry water from the public fountains.

The streets separating the insulae were so narrow that the balconies of one building almost touched those of the building across the street. Walking down the street could be nearly impossible, as vendors and wares spilled out onto the streets. The constant clatter of people, carts, and horses filled the air, as did the smell of the sewage and waste that residents threw into the streets.

Insulae did not have stoves, so plebeians cooked over open fires in *braziers*. Their diet was simple. Most ate porridge (boiled grain), bread, olive oil, and vegetables. They might occasionally add meat as well. During the first century B.C., the government began to provide free grain to poor citizens living in the city of Rome. This led many

Did You Know?

———

ROMAN BATHS WERE

SO LARGE THAT SOME

COULD HOLD UP

TO 3,000 PEOPLE

AND FEATURED A

GYMNASIUM, LIBRARIES,

AND BOTH HOT AND

COLD POOLS.

———

farmers to leave the countryside for the city, creating even more crowded conditions there.

The government also provided free entertainment in the form of gladiator games and *chariot* races. The grain handouts and entertainment were meant to keep the masses happy so that they would not riot. This led critics to believe that the plebeians cared only about "bread and circuses." Senators, equestrians, and even the emperor could be seen at the gladiator games and chariot races as well, though. The upper classes had front-row seats to such spectacles, while the plebeians sat behind them.

Over time, a few plebeians were successful enough to earn a place in those front-row seats. A plebeian who did well in business might eventually earn enough money to qualify for the equestrian class. Despite their success, such men were often looked down upon by the wealthy whose ranks they wished to join. The majority of plebeians, however, remained poor their entire lives.

Thanks to mineral springs walled in by the Romans, the English city of Bath was born.

AT THE BOTTOM

Despite their low social status, even the poorest plebeians were not at the bottom of Rome's social *hierarchy*. That position was held by slaves and freedmen. For much of Rome's history, it also included noncitizens. During the early years of the republic, noncitizens were forbidden from wearing a toga and instead wore only a tunic. This made it easy to distinguish them from the rest of the population. Noncitizens were not allowed to marry citizens. Although noncitizens were expected to pay taxes and obey Roman laws, they could not hold positions in the Roman government.

Initially, only people living in Rome could become Roman citizens. Those living in the Italian countryside

Romans of all classes were entertained by gladiator contests—but slaves were often used as fighters.

or in other Roman provinces were noncitizens. This meant that only a minority of the republic's population held Roman citizenship. In 89 B.C., anyone living in the Italian peninsula was granted citizenship. Even so, by the time the empire began in 27 B.C., 90 percent of the empire's population was still made up of noncitizens. In A.D. 212, all free peoples living in the Roman Empire were granted citizenship.

One set of people, however, remained noncitizens throughout Rome's entire history: slaves. Historians believe that there were few slaves in Rome prior to the third century B.C. Then, as Rome began to conquer new lands, it took slaves from among the conquered peoples. Both men and women—most of whom had been free before the Roman takeover—were made slaves. Other slaves were prisoners of war, rebels who fought against Roman rule, criminals convicted of serious crimes, or people who owed large debts. Sometimes people were kidnapped or captured by pirates and sold as slaves. If parents did not have enough money to feed their children, they

Did You Know?

———

USED FOR CHARIOT

RACES, ROME'S

CIRCUS MAXIMUS

COULD SEAT UP TO

250,000 PEOPLE.

TWELVE CHARIOTS

COULD RACE

AT ONCE.

———

might sell them into slavery. Other children were born into slavery. If a child's mother was a slave, that child was automatically a slave as well.

Most of Rome's slaves were from lands outside the city of Rome. On the Greek island of Delos, up to 10,000 slaves were sold to slave dealers each day. The dealers brought the slaves to Rome, where they were forced to stand naked in the slave market so that the wealthy could choose the strongest-looking slaves to run their households, manage their farms, and work in their businesses. Historians estimate that by the end of the republic, there were more than one million slaves in the Italian peninsula, making up about one-third of the Italian population.

The use of slaves meant that the wealthy did not have to spend their time working. Instead, they were free to govern the city. The kinds of work slaves did depended on where they lived. Rural slaves usually worked on a farm, planting, digging, plowing, harvesting, and tending to livestock. Trustworthy slaves might manage a portion of their owner's properties.

Now a park, Rome's Circus Maximus was once the site of chariot races and other games.

Did You Know?

DURING THE LATE

REPUBLIC, A SLAVE

NAMED SPARTACUS

LED A PARTICULARLY

FAMOUS REVOLT.

REBELLIOUS SLAVES

WERE OFTEN CRUCIFIED.

City slaves, on the other hand, usually saw to the running of a wealthy owner's household. They might serve as cooks, barbers, butlers, waiters, maids, gardeners, and dressmakers. Some worked in their master's workshops and stores, creating and selling crafts and goods. The most highly educated slaves—usually from Greece—copied books for the libraries of the wealthy or served as tutors, musicians, or artists. Some slaves were owned by the Roman government. They were put to work in building roads, aqueducts, and buildings; cleaning the public baths or temples; or keeping records.

Because they were not citizens, slaves had no rights. Legally, they were the property of their owners. In return, most slaves were provided with food and a place to sleep. Household slaves were also given gifts of money from time to time. However, most slaves were still poor.

In addition to enjoying financial gifts, slaves serving in a city household were generally treated more kindly than rural slaves. Since they lived with the families they served, they had more direct contact with their masters and mistresses, who sometimes came to regard them as friends or even as part of the family. Rural slaves, on the other hand, rarely got to know their masters. They toiled on the land from sunup to sundown, with little time for rest.

Rural slaves often faced harsher discipline than their urban counterparts as well. But all slaves could be whipped if they displeased their owner. Some owners branded their slaves or forced them to wear collars that showed to whom they belonged. A master even had the right to kill his slave. In contrast, if a master were found murdered, all of his slaves could be executed if it was suspected that one of them might be the murderer.

Some slaves tried to run away to escape such harsh conditions. Those who were caught might be sold as gladiators. After training at a gladiator school, they would be forced to fight one another—often to the death—in an arena as thousands of spectators watched. Other slaves entertained the masses as drivers in chariot races.

Successful gladiators and chariot drivers enjoyed immense popularity and could become wealthy. Like other slaves, they could be freed. A freed slave was known as a freedman or freedwoman. Some scholars believe that the majority of Rome's plebeians consisted of freedmen.

Slaves could be granted freedom in a number of ways. Some saved the money they were given by their masters and then purchased their freedom. Otherwise, friends or family members of the slave might purchase his or her freedom. Sometimes slaves were set free by their masters as a reward for their service. An owner might also set a female slave free in order to marry her.

Ancient historians described Spartacus as a former Roman soldier turned gladiator.

Child slaves might be freed to be adopted as **heirs**. Sometimes slaves who were too old to work were freed because the owner did not want the burden of providing for them.

Freedmen usually became the clients of their former master. They were expected to remain loyal and to work for him an agreed upon number of days each year. Some freedmen became paid employees of their old master, continuing to perform the jobs they had done as slaves. In turn, they had to purchase their own food and housing.

Other freedmen went on to work at new jobs, often using the skills they had developed as a slave. Most freedmen worked with and performed the same kinds of labor as other plebeians. Like the majority of plebeians, most freedmen scraped out a living and remained poor their entire lives. A few, however, became wealthy, often by working as bankers or investors. They might even have their own slaves or become patrons to their own set of clients.

Did You Know?

———

THE MARBLE COLUMN

OF TRAJAN IN ROME

IS A 125-FOOT-TALL

(38 M) MONUMENT TO

THE MILITARY VICTORIES

OF EMPEROR TRAJAN

(REIGNED A.D. 98–117).

———

Some wealthy freedmen tried to gain the respect of the upper classes by funding temples or other public buildings. But no matter how wealthy they became, freedmen were generally still scorned by the upper classes, who saw them as greedy copycats. The wealthy, freeborn men of Rome did not form social relationships with wealthy freedmen. The only contact between the two groups was often the patron-client relationship, in which the freeborn remained superior.

Although freedmen were granted citizenship and could vote, they did not enjoy equal rights with freeborn Romans. Until 18 B.C., freedmen and freedwomen could not marry freeborn citizens. After that time, a freedwoman could not marry a senator. Freedmen could never hold government offices. A freed slave's children, however, could hold important political positions. By the first century A.D., many senators and equestrians were likely descended from freedmen.

Trajan's Column is decorated with scenes from the wars between Rome and a land called Dacia.

END OF THE EMPIRE

Eventually, the Roman Empire became too large to manage all its lands and peoples. The Romans considered anyone living outside the empire a barbarian. Beginning in the middle of the third century A.D., the Romans faced repeated invasions from barbarian tribes on the borders of the empire.

Roman soldiers stationed on the frontiers to fight these barbarians often felt little connection to the emperor ruling in the far-off capital. Their loyalty was to their commanding officers. As the military gained power, successful military generals found themselves named emperor by their troops. A series of 19 men were named emperor and then quickly overthrown by the next *usurper* between A.D. 235 and 284. Such

Barbarian tribes in Germany and elsewhere fought against Roman expansion.

rapid turnover weakened the empire further, making it more vulnerable to continuing barbarian attacks.

In A.D. 395, the Roman Empire split into the Eastern and Western empires. Barbarians seized Rome in 476, leading to the collapse of the Western Roman Empire. The empire in the east continued until 1453, but it was now known as the Byzantine Empire.

The lands that had once been part of the Western Roman Empire were divided under the rule of various barbarian kings. Most of them entered a period of nearly continual warfare. The bustling cities set up by the Romans disappeared as most people returned to a rural lifestyle.

Despite the disappearance of the empire, Roman culture continued to thrive in some places. Today, the influence of Roman culture can still be felt throughout the lands it once ruled—and even farther. The Latin language spoken by the Romans directly influenced the development of many modern European languages, including Italian, French, and Spanish. In addition, the Christian religion, which had come to dominate Rome by the end of the empire, took hold in Europe. Many modern governments, including that of the United States, are still based in part on the Roman republic. Modern architecture also reveals Roman influence in such features as its arches, domes, and columns.

Today, ruins from the Roman civilization can be found across Europe, North Africa, and the Middle East, from the city of Rome to its far-flung provinces, such as Great Britain and Libya. Those ruins—along with writings from the time—reveal a complex culture made up of many people. Although those people were divided into rigid social classes, together they formed the unique society now known as ancient Rome.

El Djem, Tunisia, features a Roman amphitheater that could have seated 35,000.

753 B.C.	—	The legendary founding of Rome by Romulus and Remus begins the Roman monarchy.
509 B.C.	—	The monarchy falls, and a republic is established.
c. 450 B.C.	—	Rome's first code of law, known as the Twelve Tables, is written.
445 B.C.	—	Marriages between patricians and plebeians become legal.
367 B.C.	—	Plebeians are allowed to become consuls.
343 B.C.	—	Rome begins to expand to the south.
287 B.C.	—	Laws passed in the plebeian assembly begin to apply to all Roman citizens.
264 B.C.	—	Rome's 100-plus years of warfare begin against the North African city of Carthage, which the Romans eventually destroy.
133 B.C.	—	Tiberius Gracchus, a Roman tribune, is killed for attempting to institute land reforms benefiting the poor.
89 B.C.	—	All free people of the Italian peninsula are granted citizenship.
88 B.C.	—	Rome falls into a series of civil wars.
73 B.C.	—	Thousands of slaves participate in a revolt led by Spartacus.
58 B.C.	—	The Roman government begins to distribute free grain to poor citizens living in the city of Rome.
27 B.C.	—	The Roman republic ends, and Caesar Augustus becomes the first emperor of the Roman Empire.
A.D. 80	—	The opening of the Colosseum in Rome is celebrated with 100 days of gladiator games.
A.D. 212	—	All free people living in the Roman Empire are granted citizenship.
A.D. 235	—	A 50-year period of military-appointed emperors begins.
A.D. 379	—	Emperor Theodosius makes Christianity the official religion of the empire.
A.D. 395	—	The Roman Empire is split into Eastern and Western branches.
A.D. 476	—	The Western Roman Empire collapses.

ALTAR: a special table used for carrying out religious rituals

APPRENTICE: someone who learns a job or craft by working under the guidance of someone with more experience

AQUEDUCTS: canals or channels used to carry water to supply a city

AUGURS: priests in ancient Rome who tried to tell the future by interpreting signs in nature

BOOTY: money or goods taken from a defeated enemy in war

BRAZIERS: metal pans used to hold burning coals

CHARIOT: a two-wheeled cart pulled by horses; it was used to carry soldiers in ancient warfare

CHRISTIANITY: a religion based on the teachings and person of Jesus of Nazareth; it professes that Jesus is the son of God, that he died for the sins of all people, and that he rose from the dead

COLONNADED: surrounded by a series of columns that are usually topped by a roof

CRUCIFIXION: a method of execution in which a person is nailed or bound to a cross

EQUESTRIAN: a member of an upper-class group in ancient Rome; the name of the class derived from the fact that its members were wealthy enough to own horses and serve in the cavalry

FRESCOES: wall paintings made by painting on top of plaster while it is still wet

GLADIATOR: someone who fought, usually to the death, against other gladiators or against animals in a Roman arena for the entertainment of a crowd

GRAMMAR: rules for the proper use of language

HEIRS: people who will inherit, or receive, money or property from another person when that person dies

HIERARCHY: a ranking, or order, into which people or things are grouped, such as from highest to lowest or richest to poorest

IMPERIAL: having to do with an empire

LITTER: a couch or seat surrounded by curtains and mounted on poles, used to carry important or wealthy people

MOSAICS: pictures made from tiny pieces of glass or stone

RHETOR: a teacher of public speaking and writing

SATIRES: traditionally, Latin literary works that criticize or make fun of someone or something

TENANT: someone who rents a home or land from the property owner

USURPER: someone who uses force to illegally take a political office from the current office holder

Baker, Simon. *Ancient Rome: The Rise and Fall of an Empire*. London: BBC Books, 2007.

Connolly, Peter, and Hazel Dodge. *The Ancient City: Life in Classical Athens & Rome*. New York: Oxford University Press, 1998.

Cowell, F. R. *Life in Ancient Rome*. New York: Penguin, 1961.

Gabucci, Ada. *Rome*. Translated by Jay Hyams. Berkeley: University of California Press, 2005.

Giardina, Andrea, ed. *The Romans*. Translated by Lydia G. Cochrane. Chicago: University of Chicago Press, 1993.

Moulton, Carroll, ed. *Ancient Greece and Rome: An Encyclopedia for Students*. Vols. 1–4. New York: Scribner's, 1998.

Shelton, Jo-Ann. *As the Romans Did: A Source Book in Roman Social History*. New York: Oxford University Press, 1988.

Treggiari, Susan. *Roman Social History*. New York: Routledge, 2002.

Websites

BBC PRIMARY HISTORY: ROMANS

http://www.bbc.co.uk/schools/primaryhistory/romans/

Learn more about the city of Rome as well as its advance across Europe and into Britain.

Play a game to dig up Roman artifacts.

THE ROMAN EMPIRE IN THE FIRST CENTURY

http://www.pbs.org/empires/romans/

Learn more about daily life in the Roman Empire. Read about the empire's beginnings,

its emperors, and its enemies. Take a quiz to find out which famous Roman you are like.

Note: Every effort has been made to ensure that the websites listed above are suitable for children, that they have educational value, and that they contain no inappropriate material. However, because of the nature of the Internet, it is impossible to guarantee that these sites will remain active indefinitely or that their contents will not be altered.